JOANNA MURRAY-SMITH

Joanna Murray-Smith's plays have been produced throughout Australia and all over the world, including *Honour* which had a public reading with Meryl Streep and was produced on Broadway in 1998, the National Theatre, London, in 2003, and in the West End in 2006. Other plays include the upcoming *Ninety*, *Bombshells*, *Rapture*, *Nightfall*, *Redemption*, *Love Child*, *Atlanta* and *Flame*, many of which have been translated into other languages and adapted for radio. Her novels include *Truce* (1994), *Judgement Rock* (2002), both published by Penguin Australia, and *Sunnyside* (2005), also published in the United Kingdom by Viking. She lives near Melbourne with her husband and three children.

Other Titles in this Series

Joanna Murray-Smith

THE FEMALE OF THE SPECIES

NICK HERN BOOKS
London
www.nickhernbooks.co.uk

A Nick Hern Book

The Female of the Species first published as a paperback original in 2008 by
Nick Hern Books Limited, 14 Larden Road, London W3 7ST

Reprinted 2009, 2010, 2011

The Female of the Species copyright © 2008 Joanna Murray-Smith
Introduction copyright © 2008 Joanna Murray-Smith

Joanna Murray-Smith has asserted her right to be identified as the author of this
work

Cover design: Ned Hoste, 2H

Typeset by Nick Hern Books, London
Printed and bound by CPI Group (UK) Ltd, Croydon, CR0 4YY

A CIP catalogue record for this book is available from the British Library

ISBN 978 1 85459 522 5

Author's Note

The Female of the Species was inspired by a single image: a feminist of a certain age in the study of her country house, at the end of a long driveway, taken hostage by an angry young woman. While the scenario of this play was inspired by the true-life incident, reported in the world press, involving Germaine Greer and a young student, the characters and story of my play are entirely imagined.

My thanks to Simon Phillips and the brilliant staff of the Melbourne Theatre Company, to director Patrick Nolan and the cast of the original production. Thanks also to the steadfast, gracious David Richenthal and to Mary-Beth O'Connor, to Guy Kitchenn and Jon Bath at Cole Kitchenn, to Nick Hern and Matt Applewhite, and to Sarah Jane Leigh and Cathy King.

Particular thanks to Roger Michell and the cast of the London production. And, as always, to Estela and Raymond.

Joanna Murray-Smith

The Female of the Species was first produced by the Melbourne Theatre Company at the Victorian Arts Centre Playhouse, Melbourne, Australia, on 26 August 2006, with the following cast:

MARGOT	Sue Ingleton
MOLLY	Bojana Novakovic
TESS	Roz Hammond
BRYAN	Peter Houghton
FRANK	Bert Labonte
THEO	Michael Carman

Director   Patrick Nolan
Designer   Dale Ferguson
Lighting Designer   Matt Scott
Composer   David Chesworth

This revised version of the play was first produced by David Richenthal and Mary-Beth O'Connor, with Nica Burns and Max Weitzenhoffer for Nimax Theatres at the Vaudeville Theatre, London, on 16 July 2008 (previews from 10 July), with the following cast:

MARGOT	Eileen Atkins
MOLLY	Anna Maxwell Martin
TESS	Sophie Thompson
BRYAN	Paul Chahidi
FRANK	Con O'Neill
THEO	Sam Kelly

Director   Roger Michell
Designer   Mark Thompson
Lighting Designer   James Whiteside
Sound Designer   Matt McKenzie

For Sophia Charles and Lucy Charlotte Gill

Characters

MARGOT MASON, *sixty-ish, handsome, impressive, a
    monster*
MOLLY RIVERS, *early twenties, bright*
TESS THORNTON, *late thirties, lost*
BRYAN THORNTON, *late thirties but very boyish, handsome,
    and thick*
FRANK, *early thirties, handsome, masculine*
THEO REYNOLDS, *sixties, dapper, handsome*

Setting

*A charming house in the country. An elegant study, filled with a
lifetime's collection of books, including a shelf dedicated to
Margot Mason's own works, such as* Madame Ovary; Hear Me
Roar: The Autobiography; Honey, I'm Homo: The Complete
Insignificance of Male Sexuality; Ugly Cheating Bastards; The
Mummy Trap; H.R.T. A.S.A.P.; Nursemaids and Warlords: The
Middle-Class Marriage; Foreplay is Forearmed; For Fuck's
Sake: Women, Sexuality and Freedom; Love and Other Four-
Letter Words. *Adding to the sense of cultivated taste and a life
well lived are beautiful rugs and paintings, art works acquired
during world travels, antiques, modern pieces – all working
beautifully but without design. The room features a large desk,
a daybed and French doors opening on to a bucolic setting. On
either side of the stage are the suggestions of open, painting-
lined hallways, one leading to the kitchen, another upstairs.*

*This text went to press before the end of rehearsals and so may
differ slightly from the play as performed.*

MARGOT MASON, *an attractive, late-middle-aged woman, elegantly and casually dressed, wanders around the study speaking on her cordless phone. On her desk is her laptop and a copy of her famous book:* The Cerebral Vagina. MARGOT *is imperious, theatrical and a show-off, but there are signs here of a certain faltering in her manic work ethic.*

MARGOT. Oh, *fuck off*!... No, *you* fuck off! *You* are the reason people say the publishing industry has gone to pot. You and your *Feng Shui for Beginners*! I mean, for Christ's sake, Theo, whatever happened to learned memoirs by men of letters?... No, no, I'm working hard. (*Lolling, enervated, on the daybed.*) I'm working *very* hard, it's just taking a little longer than I thought... Haven't you got some little hack scribbling chick-lit from some Irish garret? Shopping. Sex. Men are hopeless. 'Juggling.' Honestly, if I hear that word one more time. Fucking *'juggling'*... I *am* working, I told you.

Ingeniously and casually divesting herself of her bra as she talks, without taking anything else off.

You'll get it when you get it... well, that's *your* problem... No, *that's your problem*... well, it's just not 'flowing'.

Her bra comes free and she flings it aside.

I'm not sure why. It's hard to put into words... yes, even for me. There's this little concept that keeps popping up, Theo: *stagnation*. There's just a tiny, tiny flicker of concern that finally I'm... Well – I'm bored by the sound of my own voice. Ridiculous, I know. Who's more interesting than *me*? I'll be in town on Thursday. There's a teeny-weeny oil I'm interested in... Sotheby's... fine. But this time don't take me anywhere cheap and ethnic... Hello?

She jiggles the buttons on the phone. Dead.

Hello?... Hell-o? Fuck.

She hangs up and walks over to her open laptop. She sits down and looks over what she's been writing. As she thinks of titles, she types them, regarding them on the screen.

The Dialectical Experiment of the Patriarchal Paradigm. Who the fuck is going to buy that? (*Thinking.*) Mmm… Something dignified, yet *au courant. Sex, Death and…* No, *The Feminine Something, The Feminine…* No… Got to get shopping in there somehow, or stilettos or lipstick… Perhaps something that enters the lexicon, some new coining: *Clitorism!* With an exclamation mark. *The Utopian Fallopian.* No. No. For God's sake, woman: think! If I could only get the title, the rest would follow! Something simple.

MOLLY. *The Female of the Species.*

MOLLY RIVERS *has entered through the French doors, a young woman somewhat kookily dressed, carrying a shopping bag.* MARGOT *gives a tiny glance, but is intent on seeing the title on her screen, typing it in immediately. She is captivated by the task at hand.*

MARGOT. *The Female of the Species.* Not bad.

MOLLY. I'm good with words.

MARGOT. *The Female of the Species.* (*Thinking.*) Surely it's been used?

MOLLY. Sometimes the simple is simply overlooked.

MARGOT. True!

MOLLY. You're working.

MARGOT. I *am* working.

MOLLY. There's a cow blocking the front door.

MARGOT (*lost in thought*). Yes, yes, a cow.

MOLLY. Just sitting there.

MARGOT (*concentrating on the screen*). Mmm, the Winfreys' cow.

MOLLY. I wandered around…

MARGOT. Yes, yes…

MOLLY. The doors were open.

MARGOT. So it seems.

MOLLY. French, aren't they?

MARGOT. French? Yes. French doors. I like my doors French.

MOLLY. Why are they?

MARGOT. Why are they?

MOLLY. French.

MARGOT. Because they're stylish, thin and... up themselves. *The Female of the Species*. Mmmm. (*Channelling a journalist*.) 'Her remarkable new best-seller, *The Female of the Species*, brilliantly extends the argument of her earlier smash-hit *Madame Ovary*.' 'The searing Number One title that has finally outsold *The Da Vinci Code*, *The Female of the Species*.' (*Beat*.) It's good.

MOLLY. It is good.

MARGOT. Clever.

MOLLY. I like it.

MARGOT (*delighted with herself*). It's amazing how I do that. If I wait for the muse, it comes.

MOLLY. But I –

MARGOT. I come through in the end – I *always* come through!

MOLLY. But I –

MARGOT. You have to *trust*! It's *always* in there!

MOLLY. But *I* thought of it.

Finally, MARGOT *looks up at her.*

MARGOT. You did?

MOLLY. Yes.

Beat.

MARGOT. Oh. Well... Are you sure?

MOLLY. Yes. I came in and I said –

MARGOT. Yes, yes! All right! It's not *that* good! But why am I
– This is my –

MOLLY. Yes, it's –

MARGOT. My house.

MOLLY. Yes.

MARGOT. My room.

MOLLY. Yes.

MARGOT. Those are my French –

MOLLY. Yes.

MARGOT. Doors.

MOLLY. Yes, they are.

MARGOT. I'm at work. I'm working and then –

MOLLY. Here I am.

   Beat.

MARGOT (*calm, but suddenly realising*). Who are you?

MOLLY. You don't…

MARGOT. *Should* I? I'm sorry, but –

MOLLY. You really don't know?

MARGOT. Have we met? The thing is, I just don't remember
anyone. I'm one of those people of whom others say, '*I've
met her a hundred times and she pretends she doesn't know
me.*' (*Full of self-justification, unaware of the awfulness.*)
But I'm *not* pretending. I'm really not pretending. I really
don't remember who they are.

MOLLY. I'm sure if you *try* –

MARGOT. *Honestly* –

MOLLY. You gave me a lift into town. In February. From the
campus. Remember? The horse on the road, you swerved.

MARGOT. Oh yes, the horse.

MOLLY. You must remember the horse?

MARGOT (*not remembering*). The horse, of course, yes.

MOLLY. That's it. You swerved.

MARGOT. Yes, I swerved.

MOLLY. I was in the car with you.

MARGOT. Now you mention it, I do remember there was
someone in the car. A student.

MOLLY. That was me in the car.

MARGOT (*not recognising her at all*). Oh yes, yes. Yes. *You* were
in the car when the horse swerved! How did you find me?

MOLLY. The internet.

MARGOT (*loving her own performance*). The internet! '*Where
did you meet?*' The internet. '*Why did your wife leave you?*'
The internet. '*Where have you been the last three years?*'
The fucking internet. Sixty years ago, it would have been
'the war'. Oh, the banality!

MOLLY. I Googled you.

MARGOT. Here I am, tucked away in the middle of nowhere. A
hundred miles from a caffè latte! Jesus Christ, no one's safe!
(*Deeply contemptuous.*) 'Googled'!

MOLLY. I took the train and then the bus and then I walked.
And here I am!

MARGOT. And here I am with a deadline.

MOLLY. The great Margot Mason's house!

Beat.

MARGOT (*confused*). Did we have an arrangement?

MOLLY. I tried. I wrote. But you said you were in the middle of
the next book. And you were –

MARGOT. Racing against the clock. That's exactly right. My
publisher's having a nervous breakdown, so I'm sprinting –

MOLLY. So I thought I'd just come.

MARGOT. I see...

MOLLY. I get an idea in my head and then –

MARGOT. Right.

MOLLY. I just follow through. Come what may. Is that wrong?

Beat.

MARGOT. Who are you?

MOLLY. Who am I? (*Beat.*) Molly. Molly Rivers.

MARGOT. Molly Rivers. I tell you what, I could make you a
    quick cup of tea – such a long way – and then call a taxi. On
    me. My dime. To the station.

Beat.

(*Uncomfortable.*) You could leave me some of your work
    and I could read it. And then get back to you.

MOLLY. After the book is done?

MARGOT. You see, it's taking rather longer than I thought. You
    can't hold a stopwatch to the intellect. Doesn't work…
    (*Detouring to her title search.*) *Stopwatch to the Intellect…
    The Intellectual Stopwatch…* A sophisticated concept together
    with something surprising: *Flaubert's Parrot. Kafka's Dick.
    Margot Mason's…* (*Unable to think.*) *Menopause.*

MOLLY. Look, I know I'm disturbing you –

MARGOT. It's the book, you see. Ordinarily, I'd be very happy
    – but fucking Theo is breathing down my neck. And to be
    honest… the book is killing me. *Killing me.* I have to be dis-
    ciplined. So, I'm afraid I'm going to have to…

MOLLY. Oh…

MARGOT. Reschedule. I'm happy to pencil you in…

MOLLY. Pencil me – ?

MARGOT. In. A month or so. Once the book's done.

MOLLY. Could I wait until you take a break?

MARGOT. No. You couldn't.

MOLLY. But I've come such a long –

MARGOT. No.

MOLLY. Just an hour or so would be –

MARGOT. You're forcing me to be rude. Which is *very* hard for me. But I'm a writer, Molly Rivers. And the first thing you should know is that a good writer's first love is their muse.

MOLLY. Of course you're right. I'm such an idiot!

MARGOT. We-ell, I wouldn't –

MOLLY. An idiot! I'm so embarrassed! I got carried away because I'm so sick of wasting time with those moribund, over-weight, dead, white males running that decrepit institution.

MARGOT (*delighted*). I'm flattered by exclusion.

MOLLY. I was overexcited. Like a silly schoolgirl! Fantasising about being here, *here*, in Margot Mason's house with Margot Mason – *the* Margot Mason!

MARGOT. My dear girl, settle down. I'm just a silly old... thinker. A silly old intellectual.

MOLLY. Don't be ridiculous! (I can't believe I'm telling Margot Mason she's ridiculous!) You're a legend.

MARGOT. Me? (*Giggling.*) A legend? *Absolument* not! I'm just a well-preserved old warhorse!

MOLLY. You've been around for ever!

MARGOT. Well, a *while*. Not for ever. I'm beginning to feel like Cher.

MOLLY. I want you to promise to forgive me, because I couldn't bear it if the woman who has shaped my life more than any other thought badly of me.

MARGOT *studies her intense, passionate demeanour.*

MARGOT (*softened by flattery*). Oh well...

MOLLY (*fully conscious of the effect*). Thank you, this has really *helped* me, I want you to know that. Because it's always bothered me how rarely women of a different genera-tion have a chance to *communicate*, you know?

MARGOT (*interested*). I suppose that's true...

MOLLY. And now you have work to do and I'll be off. Goodbye and good luck!

MARGOT. Well, listen – hang on a moment. There's no real rush. The publishers have waited eighteen months, they can wait an hour or so more.

MOLLY. No, they can't!

MARGOT. Yes, they can!

MOLLY. No, they can't! They can't!

MARGOT (*irritated*). *Sit down!*

MOLLY *gingerly returns to the sofa and sits down.*

(*Enjoying the discovery.*) It's good for me to be surprised. Here I am, with my little rituals, my dull routines, and it's important for me to experience the day as something – not entirely predictable. I can see you're impetuous! I love that! I adore impetuous! Listen, Molly, it's good to have you here. *Really.* To be honest, and just between us, it's just not surging forth like the last one.

MOLLY. *Nursemaids and Warlords: The Middle-Class Marriage.* It got people a bit worked up.

MARGOT. Threatened, baby. *Threatened.*

MOLLY. You've said it all, haven't you?

MARGOT. Darling, there's nothing like a hefty mortgage on an Umbrian hideaway to help you find one more publishable thought.

MOLLY. You've covered so much ground since your early pieces on sexuality and gender relations –

MARGOT. Hello, Fame!

MOLLY. Then there was reproduction. Celibacy. Cultural eradication. Menopause. Personal identity. Geriatric eroticism –

MARGOT. Oh!

MOLLY. No?

MARGOT. Geriatric! Darling, I know I'm old. I remember when a Brazilian was a *person*, but sixty is the new forty and all that.

MOLLY. Your cerebral transcendence.

MARGOT *returns to the title problem, looks back at her desk.*

MARGOT. *Cerebral Transcendence*? If only I hadn't already written *The Cerebral Vagina*! I should never have used up 'cerebral' that early. Unless… What about: *Transcendence: The Vagina Returns*.

MOLLY. You've had a huge influence on so many women. I know from personal experience, me, my mother –

MARGOT. Your mother?

MOLLY. My dead mother.

MARGOT. *Dead Mothers: The Feminist Bequest*. What do you think? Bit of a downer?

MOLLY. I've had a lot of very difficult experiences –

MARGOT (*uninterested*). Difficult, difficult, everything is so difficult!

MOLLY. I was working for a while in a Moroccan café where I was sexually molested by the owner.

MARGOT (*lightly*). Who *hasn't* been sexually molested, I ask you? I know women who have been in therapy because they *weren't* sexually molested. 'What was wrong with *me*,' they say?

MOLLY. My mother died of her own volition under the wheels of a train.

MARGOT (*throwaway*). Terrible, awful, ghastly.

MOLLY. Clutching a book.

MARGOT (*self-adoring*). What a remarkable image. The auto-didact auto-dies. Listen to me! Madam Wordplay.

MOLLY. 'You can find yourself in the truth or lose yourself in lies, but you can never find yourself in lies.'

MARGOT (*flattered*). Well done!

MOLLY. They used that line on the cover, didn't they?

MARGOT. Yes, of the first edition. Later editions simply had Isabel Allende.

MOLLY. Declaring you a genius.

MARGOT (*pleased*). Oh well.

MOLLY. And *you* said *she* was a genius for *her* book...

MARGOT. Well, ye-es –

MOLLY. How is she? Isabel Allende.

MARGOT. Dear girl, it's 'Ay-enday'. Nothing tells you more about a person than how you pronounce a writer's name. I suppose you say 'Co-et-see'. Or 'Curtsy', darling. Like what you do when you meet the Queen. It's 'Curt-see-ah' – get it right! (*With meticulous, theatrical pronunciation.*) Kazuo Ishiguro. Kenzaburō Ōe. Gao Xingjian.

MOLLY. 'Ayenday.' Thank you so much! She's fantastic!

MARGOT. Marvellous, yes. Marvellously... marvellous. Full of... marvelosity. But if you ask me, no genius.

MOLLY. *The Times* had you as number two in the Most Influential Living Women poll.

MARGOT. Polls! So silly. And vulgar. Besides which, it was only a matter of twelve votes. It's awfully cheeky of me to say it, but I do think I've been much more enduring than the others.

MOLLY. La Paglia?

MARGOT. Intellectual pornstar! Faludi, Fallaci – they all sound like a bowl of pasta. 'I'll have the Faludi with pesto.' Naomi Big-Hair accusing octogenarians of feeling her up – good God! There was no one like me! I was *outrageous* and, frankly, feminism needs theatricality or it's just one big pompous whinge.

MOLLY. I've read everything you've ever written!

MARGOT. Oh dear!

MOLLY. Even *Charlotte Brontë: Traitor From Within.*

MARGOT. That was from before you were born!

MOLLY. I *loved Jane Eyre* until I read that. But then I realised how I'd been manipulated by bourgeois notions of 'heaving bosom' literature.

MARGOT. I may have rather overstated things back then.

MOLLY. That was very funny when you said it should have been called *Jane Eyre-Head.*

MARGOT. Have you finished? Your degree?

MOLLY. Dropped out. Wanted to be a writer. Not talented.

MARGOT. Oh, so few are. But how wise, how marvellously wise to *know* you're not talented. I admire that! Oh, how I admire that! Did I actually – *teach* – ?

MOLLY. 'Feminism and Fiction.' Last year.

MARGOT (*not remembering at all*). Oh yes. Yes. Of course. You were a bright spark.

MOLLY. No, I wasn't.

MARGOT. Well, really, who cares? I mean, the academies are supermarkets these days. Shop for your degree. Aisle six, postmodern literary theory; aisle seven, detergents, breakfast cereal and an MA in Skateboarding. I feel like grabbing young women and shaking them. Get out there and find a revolution! Cry! Scream! Agitate!

MOLLY. You didn't really like my writing.

MARGOT. What a bore. But to be brutal – isn't it better to know, than to waste years attempting to be something that's just not right for you?

MOLLY. Well, what if you just haven't got there yet?

MARGOT. Got there? Darling, how long does the world have to wait? Mozart composed his first whatsit at two-and-a-half! When it comes to talented, you *are* or you *aren't.*

MOLLY. Oh.

MARGOT. So you dropped out and now – ?

MOLLY. I'm waitressing. A bit of casual nude modelling.

MARGOT. Gosh. 'Exotic.' I love the way they call it exotic when it's just a bunch of little local girls dancing on bars. I suppose that's where it all is now, the 'front line'. The whole ironic up-ending of the sexual objectification of women. You're just throwing it back in their faces, aren't you? You're just saying, 'Exploitation is in the eye of the beholder.' It's all very Third Wave.

MOLLY. Whatever…

MARGOT (*ignoring this*). You know, struggle is what makes us great. No one who's lead a cushy life comes to anything.

MOLLY. Have you struggled?

MARGOT. Me? Darling, *only all the time*! It's not easy caring so deeply about the world. I know that sounds pretentious. But I do care. *And it's exhausting.*

MOLLY. Do writers feel things more deeply?

MARGOT. What do you think?

MOLLY. I think they're good at faking it.

MARGOT (*covering her momentary unease*). I do adore the cynicism of youth! It's so crisp! But perhaps you're right. Perhaps words have taken the place of feelings. I'll have to watch that if I ever write this book –

MOLLY. I'm holding you up!

MARGOT. You're not holding it up, my dear. It's me. I'm – (*Stops herself.*)

MOLLY. You're – ?

MARGOT. It's just that I'm –

MOLLY. Yes?

MARGOT. I'm having just a…

MOLLY. A – ?

MARGOT. A touch…

MOLLY. A touch – ?

MARGOT. Of trouble… bringing it all together. There. I've said it.

MOLLY. When is it due at the publishers?

MARGOT. Yesterday.

MOLLY. How much have you written?

MARGOT. Last count… Hmmm… Including the 'ands' and 'thes'… Two-hundred-and-twenty-three words. (*Beat.*) What if I've said all I have to say?

MOLLY. I'm sure that's not so.

MARGOT. But, *what if?* I can't for ever be hauled out for television talk shows like some relic of a bygone era of political urgency –

MOLLY. Maybe you *need* a crisis of confidence.

MARGOT. Need one?

MOLLY. The humility of it.

Beat.

MARGOT (*disturbed*). Interesting.

MOLLY. Perhaps writer's block is God's way of saying, 'Take stock of yourself.' It's time to shake your ego up a little. Humility can be revitalising.

MARGOT (*shocked by this*). Oh! Well. That's all very Buddhist and everything, all very Yin and Yang, but not, perhaps, totally relevant to oneself. (*Recovering.*) Anyway, for God's sake, don't call *The Times*!

MOLLY. People change their lives because of you. Do you believe it all, or is it just the thrill of creating a storm?

MARGOT. *Oh, Molly, Molly, Molly.* Of course there's a place for provocation, for throwing a grenade every so often. These days the universities are populated with terrified men and women, desperate to hang on to their jobs at any cost. Sycophants sitting in their comfy little offices, safe in the knowledge that the powers-that-be love them because they never say anything that's going to create trouble. And these are the very people society has depended on to ask the questions that make us test the structures of our lives. If *they* don't ask the hard questions, *who will*? The new academics are lily-livered little bureaucrats cocooned in their Subaru Outbacks! –

MOLLY. Isn't it also about keeping a little industry going? The Margot Mason Industry? The whole schtick?

MARGOT (*slight askance*). 'Schtick'? Spotlighting injustice to make the world more honest? Is that 'schtick'?

MOLLY. Wouldn't you say that, in a sense, you've dragged society around in the wake of your personal revelations?

MARGOT. 'Dragged society around'? What are you saying?

MOLLY *selects each book as she cites it and drops them casually to the floor with increasing aggression.*

MOLLY. In the first book, you advocated women's liberation through the rampant freeing of their sexuality.

MARGOT. In a nutshell.

MOLLY. And then you wrote that *celibacy* was really the only way to go. Women's sexual freedom was impeding their intellects.

MARGOT. A little more complex than that, but –

MOLLY. Then there was the declaration that women should forgo babies in order to develop their brains –

MARGOT. Yes.

MOLLY. Followed by your impassioned treatise that the only path to real womanhood was in having babies.

MARGOT. Mmm…

MOLLY. Then I think you wrote in the early book that women should ditch their children in unhappy relationships –

MARGOT. Well, I was young and –

MOLLY. And the memoir insisted good mothering was the genetic blueprint for a successful life –

MARGOT. Molly, I –

MOLLY (*with a huge book*). I believe you wrote originally that men were awful.

MARGOT. I got something right!

MOLLY (*building with intensity and hostility*). Then that men were fabulous. Men are only good for sex. Feminism is just beginning. Feminism is over. Feminism is a holy war. I am feminism. I was never feminism. Feminism is fucked.

Long beat. MARGOT *stands absolutely still as she finally realises the extent of* MOLLY*'s rage.*

What happens to the women who change their lives on the basis of your declarations?

MARGOT (*alert*). They... catch up.

MOLLY. And if it's too late?

MARGOT. My dear girl, I am not a life coach. I'm a *provocateur.*

They stare at each other. Long beat.

Molly, thank you for visiting me. But now, I really think I'd better –

MOLLY. But I'm not finished.

Beat.

MARGOT. What exactly did you come here for?

MOLLY. I want an apology!

MARGOT. For what?

MOLLY. Everything!

MARGOT. *I don't apologise!*

MOLLY *pulls out a gun and aims it at* MARGOT.

MOLLY. Sit down!

MARGOT (*terrified*). Okay now. Now, just hold on. It's all okay.

MOLLY. I know it's okay.

MARGOT. It's *okay*.

MOLLY. It's okay. Okay? All right. *It's okay.*

MARGOT. It's going to be fine.

MOLLY. It *is* fine. It's fine because –

MARGOT. Because nothing has happened yet.

MOLLY. Because *I've got the gun*. That's why it's fine. I've got the gun. And I'm going to kill you.

MARGOT. Molly. Now, Molly. Calm down.

MOLLY (*not*). I'm very calm. Very.

MARGOT. No harm has been done. Not a thing. If you put the gun away and leave now, not a single thing is amiss.

MOLLY. I'll have to shoot you first.

MARGOT. Don't shoot me!

MOLLY (*lifting the gun*). I'm shooting you!

MARGOT. No!

MOLLY. I'm shooting! I'm on the verge of shooting!

MARGOT. How near the verge?

MOLLY. *Very* near the verge!

MARGOT. Molly. Molly. Be sensible. You do *not* want to do this.

MOLLY. I've wanted to do this for a very long time! *And I'm not the only one.*

MARGOT. You're upset. I shouldn't have hurried you. Why don't you put the gun away and we'll have a chat?

MOLLY. Oh, I'd love a *chat*!

MARGOT. Listen, it's the *countryside*. Sound *travels*. Last week, Veronica Talbot left her whistling kettle on the stove while she chopped the wood and *I heard it*. That was twenty miles away.

MOLLY. You think I'm stupid, don't you?

MARGOT. Look, I don't understand what your grudge is! I'm a writer and a teacher. I do the best I can. I'm honest.

MOLLY. You're not honest. You get high on your own charisma.

MARGOT. It's very hard not to! *Think* about it!

MOLLY. Okay, that's it! (*Taking aim.*) On the count of three. One –

MARGOT. No!

MOLLY. Two!

MARGOT. Don't shoot!

MOLLY (*lowering the weapon*). Look at you! You hypocrite! You nourish your little book deals, you pose nude for photographs to show what an old hipster you are, carry on about global human rights. But look at you! *What do you care about?*

MARGOT. What *don't* I care about! I care about *humanity*.

MOLLY. My life is ruined because of you.

MARGOT. Oh, *how*? Blame, blame, blame. The cult of victimhood!

MOLLY. You *started* the cult of victimhood!

MARGOT. I said, '*Take charge of your destiny!*' Listen, Molly. I'm sure you have good reasons to be angry. But *I'm not your problem*.

MOLLY. 'Go for it,' you said. You said, 'Women should act first, think later.'

MARGOT. That was deliberately facetious.

MOLLY. Women should 'stifle doubt, seize the energy of our emotions and storm the barricades of the established order.' Well, you *are* the established order.

MARGOT. That was rhetoric!

MOLLY. It was all rhetoric! You told women that if they were unhappy they should just dump their kids!

MARGOT. I was young. I *had* to go to extremes because of who I was fighting. Look, why don't you tell me what went wrong?

MOLLY. You stole my mother from me!

MARGOT. What nonsense! I can't be held accountable for the actions of women who happened to be impressionable at the very time I happened to be vocal!

MOLLY. She believed in you!

MARGOT. Nobody abandons a child because of something they *read*.

MOLLY. Oh, so you dedicated your life to trying to change people and then take no responsibility for the changes they made.

MARGOT. Look, Molly – don't you have a friend you can talk to? A family member?

MOLLY. That's great coming from you! What was it you said, 'Self-sufficiency is female Viagra'?

MARGOT. I covet independence. Is that wrong?

MOLLY. You don't need anyone, do you? Not friends. Not even family.

MARGOT. My daughter has her own life to get on with.

MOLLY. She's –

MARGOT. What she needs to be.

MOLLY. What does that mean?

MARGOT. She's made her choices.

MOLLY. But you –

MARGOT. She's a wife and mother.

MOLLY. How awful for you! You must lie in bed at night wondering what you did wrong!

MARGOT. *I wrack my brains!* What happened? I did the best I could! That girl had everything! And now… bored and boring. *Nice* husband. *Lovely* kids. *Comfortable* house. (*Beat. Without irony.*) *What sort of life is that?*

MOLLY. What does she think of you?

MARGOT. She *envies* me, Molly. How could she not? And I suspect she thinks she failed me. She was a very bright girl who just got scared.

MOLLY. What was she scared of?

MARGOT. Of being something more than mediocre. *Mediocrity*, how I loathe it! Tess has sacrificed every small thing that has ever been interesting about her.

MOLLY. So much for unconditional –

MARGOT. There's no such thing as unconditional love. Mothers are more conditional than any other creatures on the planet. You use anything you can to make that human being you've created embrace its own potential and reflect glory on you: encouragement, love, money, discipline – then moving right along to stealth, manipulation and emotional blackmail. There's nothing wrong with that. It's the way it's always been. My daughter had a chance and she blew it. You have a chance –

MOLLY. A chance to – ?

MARGOT. To own your own fate. You can walk away right now. You can go back to being whoever you used to be before you walked through these French doors. Or you can fire that gun and the rest of your life will be captive to me. You'll be the girl who brutally assassinated Margot Mason. You'll be bolstering my power, even in death. Is that really what you want?

MOLLY. I want to get back what you've caused me to lose.

MARGOT. What have you lost?

Beat.

MOLLY. Sit down! There!

MOLLY *throws the handcuffs to* MARGOT.

Put those on! Not like that, like this!

MOLLY *handcuffs* MARGOT *to the desk and then ties a scarf around her mouth, gagging her. She pauses for a second with a flicker of concern.*

(*Fixing the gag.*) Is that all right?

MARGOT (*assenting*). Mmffff.

MOLLY *goes towards the kitchen, pauses and turns around.*

MOLLY. Don't go anywhere in that chair.

MOLLY *exits.* MARGOT *sits in the chair, contemplating her situation.* MARGOT *climbs onto the desk, trying to find a way of breaking the grip of the handcuffs. She swings her legs over and finds herself precariously and comically positioned with the corner of the desk between her legs – a not altogether unpleasant sensation.*

TESS THORNTON, *an attractive thirty-something-year-old, bizarrely dressed (as if she has just put on any old thing that came to hand), comes into the room via the French doors. She absorbs the sight of* MARGOT, *cuffed and gagged, the books chaotically spread over the floor, the sound of* MOLLY *noisily banging around in the kitchen. Beat.*

TESS. I've come at a bad time. (*Beat.*) Oh dear. Look, it's fine. I mean – no value judgements. Everyone's into something, right? Really, Mum, it's okay. You're a grown woman and you want to have some fun, and why shouldn't you? It's really not that pathetic and disgusting and ugly for women your age to have – to (*Struggling with her repulsion.*) – engage intimately – to – Bryan and I find the Missionary Position challenging enough – in fact, our favourite position is the Sleeping Position – but you're perfectly entitled to... Anyway, I just want to go to my room and lie down. I swear I'll be as quiet as a mouse.

MARGOT. Mmmffffff! –

TESS. My room's still there, isn't it?

MARGOT. Mmmffffff! –

TESS. I mean, you haven't converted it, have you? Into a dungeon or something? No. All right. I'm just so tired!

MARGOT. Mmmffffff! –

*MOLLY can be heard rattling around in the kitchen.
MARGOT implores her with her eyes. TESS loosens
the gag.*

(*Fast, desperate.*) This isn't a game, this is real.

TESS. What's real?

MARGOT. There's someone here trying to kill me, Tess.
They've cut the phone line.

TESS. There's someone trying to kill you?

MARGOT. With a gun!

TESS. There's a cow blocking the front door.

MARGOT. Tess!

TESS. Is it sick?

MARGOT. Tess! I'm begging you! She's coming! Quick, hide!

*The sound of MOLLY approaching. TESS replaces the gag
and retreats, grabbing a heavy stone bust/statue. MOLLY
enters with some drinks. TESS freezes.*

MOLLY. I made tea for myself. You'll have to drink water.
Through a straw.

*She pours herself a cup of tea. Puts the glass of water in
front of MARGOT. MOLLY pulls the gag off MARGOT's
mouth. MARGOT is relieved to see TESS in her peripheral
vision, armed with the bust, approaching MOLLY with her
arms aloft, about to bring the bust down on her head.*

So, what is it about your daughter that you find so mediocre?

*TESS suddenly suspends the bust in mid-air above
MOLLY's head. MARGOT cannot look at TESS, because to
do so would give her away.*

MARGOT. I didn't say that.

MOLLY. Oh yes, you did.

MARGOT. *No, I didn't!*

MOLLY. Not ten minutes ago. A 'loser', you said.

Over the following exchange, TESS *gradually lowers the bust and retreats, backwards.*

A nappy-addled brain. Gone to mush. Major disappointment. Bored and boring. Appalling lack of –

MARGOT (*annoyed and terrified*). *All right!* I believe that her life is very different from mine. I wouldn't want hers – although it's a perfectly fine life in itself – and she wouldn't want mine.

MOLLY. But you indicated that she – how did you put it? 'Had abandoned any small thing that had ever been interesting about her.'

MARGOT (*panicking*). Well, that was unkind and untrue. She's a very bright and lovely woman, who has chosen to be a wife and mother, which is a… terrific thing. Lovely. Terrific. And it's a free world.

MOLLY (*perplexed*). You've certainly changed your tune.

MARGOT. I can say some unfortunate things at times.

MOLLY. You said, in our tutorial, that your daughter had been 'a traitor to her potential'.

MARGOT. *I'm sure I didn't say that!*

MOLLY. 'A traitor to her potential,' you said. I remember distinctly. The brutality.

MARGOT. Oh, the *brutality*. A tiny little criticism! What cissies we've all become!

MOLLY. You used her as a warning of what might happen to us if we failed to, quote, respond to our intellectual momentum, unquote. You said we'd stagnate in a sea of domestic passivity, blowing other people's noses for the rest of our lives.

MARGOT (*arch*). Well?

MOLLY. I'm suddenly absolutely starving. Got anything in your fridge that I can pronounce?

MARGOT. Probably not.

MOLLY. Make a noise and I'll just pop back and shoot you in the heart.

MOLLY *leaves the room.* MARGOT *turns to look at* TESS, *who is staring at her mother in silence. Long beat.*

MARGOT. I shouldn't have said those things.

TESS *says nothing.*

And we can talk about it. We can certainly talk about it, Tess. But not right now. We don't have much time. You have to go to the Winfreys' and call the police.

TESS *doesn't move.*

Tess, I'm begging you! I know you must be angry, but for God's sake. I could be murdered!

TESS. *You told your class?*

MARGOT. She's exaggerating!

TESS. You used me as a *cautionary* tale?

MARGOT. Tess, you have to call the police! She's going to be back in a minute!

TESS. I can't believe you'd do that! I've 'abandoned any small thing that has ever been interesting about me'?

MARGOT. Tess, *we can talk about this later*!

TESS. I want to talk about it now!

MARGOT. There's a maniac on the loose and you want to talk about ideology?

TESS (*sniffling*). No. (*It's a historical refrain between them.*) I want to talk about *me. Your* attitude to *me.* You don't love me!

MARGOT. Tess!

TESS. *You don't love me! You've never loved me! I'm exhausted!*

MARGOT. Of course I do!

TESS. Well, say it then!

MARGOT. I don't need to say it!

TESS. Say it! Say the word!

MARGOT. It's a silly, hackneyed word!

TESS. When have you *ever* used it?

MARGOT (*this is her worst nightmare*). Tess!

TESS. *When?*

MARGOT. Of course I have... (*Wracking her brains for an example and then triumphant.*) Fromage.

TESS (*disbelieving*). *Fromage?! The fucking dog?!*

MARGOT. As an example.

TESS. *Say it!*

MARGOT (*total, total nightmare*). Help me, Tess.

TESS (*suddenly hard*). *Fuck you.*

> *They both jump at this.* TESS *takes a long slug from the Scotch bottle.*

> You never came to Lily's *Alice in Wonderland*!

MARGOT (*this, again!*). For Christ's sake, she wasn't even *Alice*. She was a fucking *teapot*!

TESS. You're her grandmother!

MARGOT. Don't use that word! You know how I feel about that word!

TESS. You told Tom that Woofy would die.

MARGOT. Well, Woofy *will* die, eventually.

TESS. And then I would die and his father would die and then eventually he himself would die and everyone in the universe would die at some stage if we weren't blown up by terrorists first.

MARGOT. Jesus! Isn't that true?

TESS. He was *four*. (*Beat.*) Who's my father?

MARGOT. Not that again!

Here it comes again. It's been 'the' issue for decades.

TESS (*loudly, so* MOLLY *will hear*). *Who's my father?*

MOLLY *enters with the gun poised.*

MOLLY. Who are you?

TESS. Who are *you*?

MOLLY. No, who are *you*?

TESS. Oh, oh, I'm the Loser.

MOLLY. The Loser?

TESS. That's me.

MOLLY. So *you're* the Loser?

TESS. Yes, I am. And now we've got that cleared up, who are you?

MOLLY. I'm a homicidal maniac!

TESS (*too tired to care*). Congratulations.

MOLLY. I'm going to have to tie you up.

TESS. You really don't need to.

MOLLY. Yes, I do.

TESS. I mean –

MOLLY. That's what –

TESS. I'm not –

MOLLY. That's what people do. In this situation. They tie people up. (*Beat.*) Move, over here.

MARGOT. She's not going anywhere!

TESS. I'm exhausted! I had to walk all the way from the main road. I got a taxi from the station. My God, those taxi fares have really – for that price you shouldn't have to listen to the driver droning on. His life story. Wife leaving. Didn't know what she wanted but knew it wasn't him, blah blah blah.

He dropped me at the end of the drive because he didn't want to get stuck in the mud. Men are so pathetic. I wish I was a lesbian. I really do. It would be so much more fun, now that they're so glamorous. (*Pondering as she surveys* MOLLY *momentarily.*) Maybe I should just try to be a lesbian. It can't be any harder than Italian. Anyway, I'm tired. I'm very tired. I need to lie down.

MOLLY. I'm about to shoot your mother and you want to lie down?

MARGOT. For God's sake, don't go all airy-fairy now!

TESS. 'Airy-fairy'? '*Airy-fucking-fairy*'??? Last night I made seventy-four shabby-chic tissue-box holders out of Corn-flakes packets and electrical wiring, does that sound like airy-fairy to you? I made two hundred and forty-nine Corn-flake Clusters for the school fête!

MARGOT. *She's got a gun,* Tess.

MOLLY (*a little annoyed*). Get your hands behind your head!

TESS. Later. I promise. But right now I'm just going to tootle upstairs for a napette.

MOLLY. For God's sake, I'm about to kill your mother!

TESS. Mmm. Yes. By all means kill her, but be fast and accu-rate. On second thoughts, I'm just going to lie myself down over here and watch, don't mind me.

MOLLY *watches her lie down.*

What is a Pokémon, anyway?

MOLLY. What is – What?

TESS. All day long. This relentless, '*Where do Pokémons go on holiday? What do Pokémons eat for snacks? Do Pokémons tan?*' How do I know? '*Does the earth go round the sun or does the sun go round the earth?*' Lily said, '*Which wins: fire or water?*' Which *does* win? I don't know anything! I don't know the difference between mammals and... the other things. They look at me like I should know. I *should* know. And because of me and my ignorance, my tiredness, they'll be heroin addicts in a couple of years, they'll be sitting dozing on public transport with pierced lips. Who is God?

MOLLY. Who is God?

TESS. I don't know.

MOLLY. Who does know?

TESS. Shouldn't I know? If mothers don't know who God is, who does?

MOLLY. What did you say?

TESS. I said, '*You* are God.'

MOLLY. Oh, that's good.

TESS. And she said, if she were God, she'd know where Pokémons went on holiday.

MARGOT (*immensely irritated*). Oh, bravo for theological chit-chat, but I'm wondering what we're going to do here? I mean, what are we doing?

TESS. Can't you shoot her? I mean, wasn't that the plan?

MOLLY. It is the plan.

TESS. So?

MOLLY. All in good time.

TESS. What's a plan good for if you don't stick to the plan?

MOLLY. What?

TESS. Show a bit of resolve, for Christ's sake. Shoot her and then shoot me.

MOLLY *studies* TESS, *baffled.*

MOLLY. *What's wrong with you?*

TESS. I told you.

MOLLY. What, you just landed on your mother's doorstep because you're sick of your kids making noise?

TESS. Oh, *okay.* That's *nothing!* That's just nothing to you, of course it is. *A little bit of noise. What is she going on about?*

MOLLY. I just meant –

TESS. On and on. All day long. I wake up in the morning and I just can't believe it. Another day on the treadmill. Relentless, never-ending noise, on my feet all day long: juice, sweater, juice, spills, school bags, projects. '*I have to make a cinema,*' he said. '*By tomorrow. To scale. In balsa wood.*' *Do I look like I make cinemas?* When I pushed him out six years ago, did I know I was going to have to make a balsa-wood cinema to scale all through the night? Huh? Huh? *Did I?* '*Mummy, mummy, mummy, mummy, mummy, mummy!*' You know, I'm human too! I have needs too! No one cares about me!

Beat as they take in the magnitude of the pain.

MOLLY (*taking charge*). Well, it seems to me, you just need a rest. Doesn't she, Margot?

MARGOT. Of course she does!

MOLLY. You just need a rest. A few days in the sun. You've just been on the go for too long. Too much pressure. Not enough sleep. You need someone to talk to. It's very isolating being a mother of young children.

Silence.

TESS (*stupefied*). How did you *know* that?

MOLLY (*with passion*). Motherhood is fundamentally underappreciated by a society that has lost touch with its primal forces.

TESS (*shocked*). Oh.

MOLLY. The elevation of the corporate sensibility in modern life, the advent of maniacal consumerism and the exaggerated elevation of professional success as the measure of a life has stymied the recognition of fundamental nurturing. No one realises that those demented-looking women staring blankly at the yoghurts in the supermarket hold *the future of the world* in the palm of their hands.

Beat.

TESS. Oh my God! You understand!

MOLLY. Of course I do! The men are still out there hunting, aren't they?

TESS. I think that's what Bryan's doing. I'm not sure. It's all about hedging.

MARGOT. Hedging his bets! Typical male!

TESS. Hedging other people's bets. It's very complicated. It's like a game show on TV, only everyone wears suits. Bryan says, 'Oil's going up' and 'HobNobs are going down' and everyone starts yelling, 'Buy! Buy! Buy!' or 'Get rid of the HobNobs! Dump the HobNobs! Dump them! Dump them!' And if Bryan's right, he makes the company millions of pounds.

MOLLY. HobNobs?

TESS. As an example.

MOLLY. Well, all right, but the point is, he's out there in the world, standing around water coolers talking about Brad and Angelina.

MARGOT. Exactly!

TESS. Is he?

MOLLY. While you're at home working on the hardest, most remarkable job on the planet, the job of making good humans.

TESS. Good humans? I think they are!

MOLLY. Bryan's just one more –

MARGOT. *Caveman –*

MOLLY. – Out there, following his base instincts, leaving you to the hard stuff and not even thinking about it, not even really understanding. That bastard!

MARGOT. *That bastard!*

TESS. He doesn't seem like a caveman. He does the ironing. Everything except the duvet covers.

MOLLY. It's too big!

TESS. I know. They're queen size.

MOLLY. *Motherhood*. (*Beat*.) I'm just saying, motherhood is underappreciated.

TESS (*acknowledging for the first time*). I'm terrible at it!

MOLLY. Of course you're not!

TESS. I am! I am! I'm terrible!

MOLLY. You're not terrible! You're just feeling very alone!

MARGOT. She's not very good.

MOLLY *and* TESS. Shut up!

TESS. I've given my life over to something I have no talent for.

MOLLY. That can't be true! How do you measure talent for mothering? *Being there*.

TESS. Well, I'm not, am I? I'm here.

MOLLY. A break isn't going to kill them. Anyway, can't their father take some responsibility?

MARGOT. Bryan – I doubt it!

MOLLY. Can't Bryan make a contribution?

TESS. Well, not right now.

MOLLY. Why not?

TESS. He's in Shanghai.

MARGOT. Of course he is!

TESS. Or Dubai.

MOLLY. Shanghai or Dubai?

TESS. That place with the money!

MOLLY. Well, who's with the kids?

TESS (*vague*). Who's with them?

MOLLY. Who'd you leave the kids with?

TESS. You're asking me?

MOLLY. Who else would I be asking! Who'd you leave the kids with?

Beat. Dawning on them all.

You left them with someone, didn't you, Tess?

TESS (*confused*). Well...

MARGOT. *Where are the children,* Tess?

TESS. I just sort of walked outside to get some fresh air.

MOLLY. You walked outside, and...?

TESS. I kept walking.

MARGOT. And then what?

TESS (*not discovering the end until she's there*). And then I thought I'd walk down the street and then I just kept going until I came to the station. And so I got on the train and then I got in the cab with the driver with the fascinating life story. And then I walked up the drive.

MARGOT. You left the kids alone! Jesus!

TESS (*realising*). My God... *My God!!!*

MOLLY (*panicking*). Okay, all right, don't panic.

TESS. *They're alone! The kids are all alone!*

MOLLY. It's okay.

TESS. The kids are alone, Molly! They're all by themselves in a house full of electrical sockets!

MOLLY. It's going to be all right, Tess.

TESS. In a neighbourhood crawling with paedophiles! Oh my God! My God! My God!

MOLLY. Oh my God! I'll call the police.

TESS. You can't call the police! They'll arrest you!

MARGOT. What do you care?!

TESS. They'll take her away!

MARGOT. Isn't that *good*?

TESS. No. I like her. She listens. And she's going to shoot you!

MARGOT. Tess!

TESS. *It's a golden opportunity!*

MOLLY. How old are they?

TESS. Tom's a very mature… six. Lily is a very sophisticated… four… And Rosie is… almost two, but seems more like… two-and-a-half.

MOLLY. Oh my God.

MARGOT. This is insane! Listen, Molly, you run to the neighbours, call the police and then go. Just go. We'll never say a thing.

TESS. If you go, I don't know what I'll do.

MOLLY. I'll e-mail the police!

MARGOT. Have you ever heard of anyone *e-mailing the police*? How many times in the movies have you heard someone say, 'If you don't get out of my house now, I'll *e-mail* the cops!'

TESS (*to* MOLLY). When are you shooting her? (*Realising*.) I have a mobile.

MOLLY. You have a mobile phone?

MARGOT. For God's sake, Tess!

TESS. I forgot. I turned it off. Can't stand the *Bob the Builder* ringtone.

MOLLY. Okay, call the cops. Now. Don't say where you are. Or I'll kill you.

TESS. Yes, yes, you'll kill me. Just like you've killed my mother *who you came to kill*.

MOLLY *grabs the phone*.

MOLLY. Hello? Police? I have reason to believe some young children have been left on their own at a house in…

MARGOT. Oxley Green. Fourteen, Willow Crescent.

MOLLY. Oxley Green. Fourteen, Willow Crescent. Yes. Never mind who I am, just get someone over there. The mother went out to buy...

TESS (*improvising*). Mustard seeds...

MOLLY. Mustard seeds.

TESS. Run over by a bus...

MOLLY. Tragically run over by a bus. She was wearing earplugs and she didn't hear it coming.

She hangs up.

They're on their way.

Beat as the three women relax.

TESS. For a homicidal maniac, you're awfully sweet.

MOLLY. I like children.

TESS. When all this is over, you can settle down and have yourself a few.

MOLLY. No. I can't have them.

Sharp intake of breath from TESS.

TESS. My God! Why not?

MOLLY. Because of *your* mother! Who wrote in *The Cerebral Vagina* that procreation was genetic masturbation.

MARGOT. For God's sake, that was a hundred years ago!

TESS (*appalled*). What?

MOLLY. Your mother wrote that 'for every child, a great novel goes unwritten'.

TESS (*horrified*). She said that?

MOLLY. *My* mother hung on her every word. She had me and gave me away.

TESS. She gave you away!

MOLLY. At birth.

TESS. *No!*

MOLLY. Never knew her. Tried to find her. Dead.

TESS (*snivelling*). Dead?

MOLLY. As a dodo.

TESS. *My God!*

MOLLY. And whose fault is it?

TESS (*furious*). *Her* fault! She did it! She's the reason you're all alone! She's the reason you'll *always* be alone in a bedsit full of old Argos catalogues and cat food! She's the reason you'll *die* alone, only discovered by a census collector years later! *She's* the reason they'll need dental records!

MOLLY. *All right. All right.*

TESS. Childless and motherless!

MOLLY. My mother died with a copy of *The Cerebral Vagina* in her hands.

TESS *and* MARGOT. Oh my God!

MOLLY. She worshipped your mother and so in honour of *my* mother, I took *your* mother's class at university.

MARGOT (*dismissive*). Oh, mothers, mothers everywhere!

MOLLY. I thought: this is the only way I can really understand my heritage. I read everything. I started with *The Cerebral Vagina* and then *Behind the Vagina*, and then I watched the four-part documentary and the dramatised adaptation, then the book about the writing of *The Cerebral Vagina – The Vagina File*s – and then last year's *Reality Vagina*.

MARGOT. The ratings went through the roof!

TESS. I hate that word. I know it's silly, I can deal with 'penises' until I'm blue in the face, and occasionally I do, but the 'V word' I just find ugly.

MARGOT. For God's sake!

TESS. Oh, that's right, humiliate me! I don't care! I think whoever named it could have done better. Why couldn't it be a 'dandelion'? Huh? Or a 'falafel'? Or even an 'ottoman'? What's wrong with that? *The Cerebral Ottoman* is much prettier.

MARGOT surreptitiously writes it down, trying it out.

MOLLY. I believed in your mother. I had an operation so that I would never conceive children.

Sharp intake of breath from TESS and MARGOT.

MARGOT. You foolish girl, any idiot knows that's not what I intended!

MOLLY. And then the first essay I wrote in her class... I wept over it! I worked long into the night, night after night. Even when I worked eighteen-hour shifts *for tips*, I got up to write and rewrite because it had to be perfection. I thought: *Margot Mason deserves perfection.* So I wrote and I wrote, I ripped it up a thousand times and finally, finally, I thought it was worthy of her. It was the story of a strange new world – like this world, only just slightly futuristic, you know, no one eats, they just swallow tiny pills that are like *virtual* chicken casserole or *virtual* chicken pie, only not just chicken – anyway, a strange new world where women get eaten by their ovaries. The enemy within.

TESS. Wow!

MARGOT (*with horrible realisation*). Oh my God, I *do* remember.

MOLLY. And I'll never forget it, the day the essays came back. She told me I had no talent. I was worthless. The great Margot Mason.

MOLLY stands, visibly upset.

TESS. You poor, poor darling!

MOLLY. I need some water.

She exits quietly to the kitchen.

TESS (*to* MARGOT). If you make a sound, I will personally chop you up into very small pieces and feed you to your fucking chickens.

TESS *follows* MOLLY *to the kitchen.* MARGOT, *stupefied by these events, sits paralysed in the chair, wildly thinking of some way out. She spies the Scotch bottle along the desk and bends, trying to grab the top of it in her mouth. When that fails, she lifts her leg and uses her foot to slide it towards her, then finds that her leg has cramped. She struggles to lift her leg and drop it on the floor. Dexterously, with her cuffed hands, she tips the Scotch into her water glass and starts to drink it through the straw. Suddenly* BRYAN THORNTON, *the handsome thirty-ish husband of* TESS, *dressed in a conservative suit and tie, enters through the French doors, breathless.* BRYAN *is the quintessential 'nice guy' – very straight, a whizz with numbers but otherwise brainless.*

BRYAN. Margot – Is she here?

MARGOT. She's here.

BRYAN. Thank God! There's a cow on your doorstep.

MARGOT. I'm aware of that.

BRYAN. Is it sick?

MARGOT. No, just stubborn.

BRYAN (*indicating handcuffs*). What are they?!

MARGOT. They're handcuffs, Bryan. What? Never chained Tess to the bedhead?

BRYAN (*momentarily confused, then*). Tess left the kids.

MARGOT. I know.

BRYAN. Just walked out.

MARGOT. I know.

BRYAN. They were home alone.

MARGOT. Are they all right?

BRYAN. Thank God, a courier found them who spoke to our neighbour who took them in. The kids had eaten three packets of sugar lumps and nine mothballs, but otherwise they were unharmed. Where is she?

MARGOT. Can you get this thing off me? I've had enough!

BRYAN. Who has the key?

MARGOT. *Who has the key? The person who handcuffed me to the desk has the key.*

BRYAN. We need an angle-grinder, Margot.

MARGOT. Thanks, Bryan, could you pop down to B&Q and get one?

BRYAN. Not now, Margot! I need to see Tess.

MARGOT. She's in the kitchen. Chatting. With a psychotic intruder.

BRYAN. The neighbours called me. Luckily, I was on my way home from the airport. She left the kids!

MARGOT. I know!

BRYAN. Margot, *she left the kids alone.*

MARGOT. I know she did, Bryan.

BRYAN. What's going on?

MARGOT. Let's see… There's a maniac in the house and my idiot son-in-law has just ridden into town on a white fucking stallion.

BRYAN (*looking around*). Where?

TESS *and* MOLLY *enter, their laughter interrupted at the sight of* BRYAN.

Tess!

TESS. Oh God, no!

MOLLY. Put your hands on top of your head or I'll shoot to kill.

MARGOT. It's just Bryan.

BRYAN *puts his hands on his head.*

BRYAN. Okay, all right, I'm not going to try anything! I give you my word.

MOLLY. You give me your word?

BRYAN. Yes, I do. And ask anyone, but that means something where I come from.

MOLLY. Where do you come from?

BRYAN (*momentarily confused*). Ahh, a place where people's word means something.

MARGOT (*to* MOLLY). I can't think of a better introduction to Bryan than that.

TESS. Are the kids all right, Bryan?

BRYAN. The kids are fine, Tess. Are *you* all right?

TESS. I'm dandy. (*Realising.*) Haven't been this good in years.

BRYAN. I was worried, Tess.

TESS. Sorry, Bryan.

BRYAN. You're my soulmate, Tess.

TESS. Soulmate. Mmm. Yes.

BRYAN. We've shared so much, Tess.

TESS. I guess so, Bryan.

BRYAN. We have a beautiful family.

TESS. Yes, we do.

BRYAN. And family is everything, isn't it, Tess?

TESS. It's a lot. But it isn't everything.

BRYAN. What's the point of existence, Tess? Without a family?

TESS. Well, there's pleasure.

BRYAN. Sure, but apart from that.

MOLLY. *Hello? Hello? I've got a gun, in case you've all forgotten.*

TESS. This is Molly, Bryan. She's an armed intruder.

BRYAN. I'm Bryan. I'm in funds.

MOLLY. I know.

TESS. Molly's a psychological wreck.

MOLLY. Well, I'm –

TESS. Mentally speaking, she's been dragged through the mill.

BRYAN. Ouch!

TESS. She's been profoundly unhinged –

MOLLY. Well –

TESS. Abandoned at birth. Unable to have children. Desperate for offspring.

BRYAN. Hell's bells!

TESS. Molly's mother gave her up at birth beause she'd been brainwashed by the Margot Mason Industry.

BRYAN. That's awful!

TESS. And then her mother, a beautiful free spirit, threw herself under a train, clutching a copy of *The Cerebral Vagina*.

BRYAN. Oh my God!

TESS. And she looked to my mother, her mentor, for solace and meaning and she showed her nothing but contempt!

MARGOT. You didn't read her essay, Tess.

TESS. Then she had an operation so she'd never have kids because for just a fleeting moment, Margot fucking Mason told women to do just that.

BRYAN. I think you can make the point without the language, Tess. But then you know how I feel about that. Tess, what's happening?

TESS. I just couldn't take the noise, Bryan. It was that simple. I finally just couldn't take it any more.

BRYAN. You left them home alone, Tess.

TESS. I want it! You had it before! It's my turn! I want it! Give it to me! Enough. No more. But they don't listen to me. Bryan, they don't listen. So I walked out of the kitchen just to get away from the noise and it suddenly seemed like a good idea to keep walking.

BRYAN. I want to take you home, Tess.

TESS. I can't go home, Bryan. Not until I know where Poké-mons go for their holidays.

MOLLY. Are the kids really okay?

BRYAN. They're fine. But why do you care?

MOLLY. People who have had awful childhoods either want to continue the cycle of suffering or they want to rewrite their history by seeing children thrive in an optimal environment.

BRYAN. You've done therapy, obviously.

MARGOT. Absolutely. That's why she breaks into people's houses and starts threatening them with firearms.

BRYAN. I don't think we need to get into *value judgements*, Margot. Value judgements are no help at all.

MARGOT. Really? I can't make a value judgement over a deranged intruder threatening my life?

BRYAN. No one makes value judgements any more, Margot. It's all culturally relative. Somewhere in the world she is totally normal. Who's to say *our* 'normal' is the only legiti-mate normal? Maybe *we're* the strange ones – ever thought about that, Margot?! (*Tapping his head.*) Sometimes you have to seal the envelope.

MARGOT (*to* MOLLY). Couldn't you shoot *him*?

MOLLY. Okay, that's it!

MOLLY *shoots at the ceiling. Everyone screams. A piece of plaster crashes to the floor. They all stop in shocked silence.*

BRYAN. Sugar! That's a real gun!

MOLLY. It's what people in the know call a loaded weapon.

BRYAN. It's a real gun, all right!

MOLLY. Next time, I shoot to kill. (*To* MARGOT.) So watch your mouth.

BRYAN. Now, Molly, you know, violence hardly ever works.

MOLLY. Oh, it works!

BRYAN. It works, but what I'm saying is, actions speak louder than words.

MOLLY. That's what *I'm* saying.

BRYAN. Oh no, no. I mean, the pen is mightier than the sword.

MOLLY. Well, according to your mother-in-law, I can't write. I have no talent. So this is my only redress.

MARGOT. For God's sake!

BRYAN. I'm just saying, don't do anything hasty. You know, revenge is a dish best eaten a long time after the dust has settled.

TESS (*finally, realising*). Bryan, I'm not coming back.

BRYAN. Don't be ridiculous. Of course you are. You have a home. You have a family. You have me. I love you, Tess.

TESS (*to* MARGOT, *bitterly*). You see, *he* can say it!

BRYAN. You *know* I've always mounted you on a pedestal.

MARGOT. Good Lord.

TESS. Do you stand around the water cooler, Bryan?

BRYAN. Do I stand around the water cooler?

TESS. Discussing Brad and Angelina?

BRYAN (*confused*). Is that wrong?

MOLLY. While you're out there, guessing on the ups and downs of things, she's manning the home front, going totally insane. Do you know how hard it is caring for three small children? Do you? *Do you?* Do you have any idea? What it's like to be trapped in the house, day after day, apprenticing

small humans in how to be civil? Not to snatch and grab?
Not to throw pasta around the room? Not to tell people
they're fat when they are? Do you know how hard that is,
Bryan, do you really know?

BRYAN. Well… Probably not. No. I probably only get a tiny
glimpse of it. I don't think I do know.

MOLLY (*shocked, deflated by this*). Oh.

BRYAN. I think most of us blokes probably have no idea just
how good women are at doing a hundred and one things at
once. Sometimes I look at Tess and she's feeding Rosie and,
and stirring the dinner and on the phone and folding the
laundry and throwing something at Tom and, and sobbing,
all at once, and I think, My God, what I do out there in the
so-called 'real world' amounts to pretty much nothing com-
pared to her and no one thanks her for it, no one thanks her
for the fact that she's raising the next generation of
humankind.

TESS, MOLLY *and* MARGOT *stare at him in silence.*

(*Building with increasing feeling to the point of a Presiden-
tial address.*) However tiring my work is – and sometimes
I'm doing seventeen-hour days – at least it's out there in the
world, part of the ebb and flow of global currents. And Tess
back home is trapped in this little micro-world of domes-
ticity and it's the tinyness of it, the banality of it, which is so
exhausting because it's simultaneously the most important
job in the world and the most invisible. (*Reaching a
crescendo.*) *These women are heroines.* And in their own
way, in charting the mystery of new lives, *they* are society's
Amelia Earharts. They are the great adventurers and by gosh,
they're doing it for all of us.

More stunned silence.

(*Embarrassed.*) You know what, I'm going to go into the
kitchen and rustle us all up something to eat. What do you
say to that?

MOLLY (*without much force*). If you try to run, I'll hunt you
down and shoot you.

BRYAN. Okey-dokey.

BRYAN *exits to the kitchen.*

MOLLY (*quietly smitten*). He's not what I expected.

MARGOT. That's what Tess said after the wedding night.

TESS. He kept asking me if I enjoyed performing Horatio.

MARGOT. Only Bryan could confuse *Hamlet* with oral sex.

TESS. Oh, all *right.*

MARGOT. Will someone give me a little credit here? Do you remember, Tess? Do you? When I took you aside and I sat you down and I said, 'I have only three words to say to you, and they may be the most important words I ever say: Boring. Boring. Boring.' But did you listen?

TESS. It was four minutes before I was supposed to be walking up the aisle.

MARGOT. '*Boring. Boring. Boring.*' You didn't have to be a rocket scientist.

TESS. I thought I wanted boring. I was sick of the kind of people I grew up around.

MARGOT. Oh, *right*! World leaders! Poets Laureate! Iris Murdoch! Derrida gave you your first solids! He broke up the rusk and gave you the pieces out of order.

TESS. I just wanted a simple guy.

MARGOT. Well, honey, *you hit the jackpot.*

TESS. Well, maybe if I'd *had* a strong, stable man in my life, I wouldn't have wanted to marry one.

MOLLY. He seems very nice.

TESS. I don't want nice. I want… *bad.* I want a man who says, '*Get undressed, I'm taking you from behind.*'

MOLLY. Well, you're never going to find one of those any more.

TESS. '*And if you don't please me, I'm going to make you clean the house in nothing but a maid's apron.*'

MOLLY. They've gone. And you've got your mother to thank for that.

TESS. *'And after I've had you, I'll have your twin sister!'*

MARGOT. *My God! What's wrong with you women?* Where's your *rage*? Here you are, surrounded by men who'll stop at nothing to patronise and condescend to you, to keep you powerless, to render you sexual handmaidens and you don't care! Young women look at ice-cream commercials with females simulating blow jobs and they think, 'That's all I'm good for.'

MOLLY. No. Young women think, 'I *enjoy* giving blow jobs and when I stop enjoying it, I'll stop giving them. And then I might climb Everest in fishnets or bake cupcakes while campaigning to be the President of Chile,' isn't that right, Tess?

TESS. All except the part about enjoying… (*Just vaguely miming a head dipping.*) You know.

MOLLY (*continuing, to* MARGOT). Your resentment does more to trip us up than any puerile slights from the male of the species. *Men* aren't our problem. *Old feminists are.*

MARGOT. My God!

MOLLY. The point, Tess, is that Bryan seems like a good person.

TESS. That's true, Molly.

MOLLY. His heart is in the right place.

MARGOT. Unfortunately his *brain* isn't.

TESS. It's good that Bryan's a decent person. Of course it's good. But it doesn't make *fire* run through my veins!

MOLLY. Maybe he *is* wildly exciting. Maybe you've just never seen that in him. Maybe he's really a depraved, perverted sex-god.

BRYAN *enters wearing* MARGOT'*s apron over his suit, carrying a tray with soup mugs.*

BRYAN. I've found some soup. We all need a nice bowl of soup and things will look much better. Sometimes I think there's nothing better than a nourishing bowl of soup. (*Sitting himself down comfortably with his soup.*) Well, you know my policy, Margot. I've never hidden it from you. I think you've made a lot of real mistakes.

MARGOT. What 'mistakes'?!

BRYAN. Too numerous to outline at this point, but you know what I'm talking about. (*With a kind of grim determination.*) Putting *ideas* ahead of *people*.

MARGOT. You think I put ideas ahead of people?

BRYAN. Yes, I do. And I'm not altogether certain it's all about the ideas either.

MARGOT. What's that supposed to mean?

BRYAN. Just you courting a certain degree of celebrity. There, I've said it. Celebrity at the expense of people's feelings.

MARGOT. Me, courting celebrity? Darling, *celebrity* courts *me*.

BRYAN. Well, you can play your fancy word games, Margot, but look at us – we've *all* suffered because of you, one way or another.

TESS. Exactly.

MOLLY (*wildly impressed*). Right on the money.

BRYAN. Take Molly. First of all, you killed her mother.

MARGOT. I never knew her mother!

BRYAN. Well, that's the point, isn't it! You never knew a lot of people.

MARGOT. What?

BRYAN. But that didn't stop you ruining their lives. Molly's mother took what you said to heart. She gave up her baby because you told her to.

MARGOT. I never told her to!

MOLLY. 'Delete dependency,' you said.

MARGOT. I didn't mean 'Give your children away!' My God, now I'm responsible for all the emotionally disturbed women out there!

BRYAN (*pleased with this thought*). Now, now, Margot, I don't think 'labels' are going to help. One person's 'emotionally disturbed' is another person's 'sensitive artist'.

MARGOT. What are you saying? That intellectuals shouldn't exercise their intellect in case it's misinterpreted!

BRYAN. Molly made sacrifices she thought were for a point. You told her they were for a point and she bought it and look where it's got her! She loves kids and she's never going to have kids. She's a beautiful, smart young woman standing in a house with a gun. She's just one more example of how society lets young people down. (*Gathering confidence.*) She started out innocent. Just a newborn. Full of hope and life. And then, one by one, the world took things away from her. Her mother. Her *dreams*. She winds up looking for a hero and she finds – Margot Mason. She turns to you, looking for a mentor who will look right into her soul and tell her she is a valuable thing. A young woman to whom the world is her lobster.

MOLLY. Oyster –

BRYAN. No, I won't thanks. (*Continuing, to* MARGOT.) And you see nothing! You have no idea at all of the responsibility at your feet! You dash off a trite response, thinking nothing of it, and there she is, a beautiful, gorgeous, intelligent... *sexy* girl, dashed on the rocks of cynicism.

MOLLY (*transfixed*). Oh my God.

BRYAN. She's probably dumped a string of good men, too – probably single right now for all I know (*Beat, as he contemplates the implications.*) – because you told her, indirectly, that her power would be diminished by... well, *love*.

MOLLY (*amazed, impressed, touched*). How did you know?!

BRYAN (*tapping his head*). Oh, there are a couple of things going on up here, Molly.

MARGOT. Yes, but *only* a couple.

BRYAN. You've never been big on love, Margot.

MARGOT. Love!

BRYAN. That's right. You think it's a hokey little concept for greeting cards. But some of us aren't afraid of feelings, Margot. We're not afraid of five little letters that make a positive difference. If that makes us sentimental or corny, well, that's okay. (*Beat, as he realises and corrects himself.*) *Four.* I'm a simple guy, Margot, and simple is as simple does.

MARGOT. What the *hell* are you talking about?

BRYAN. I'm talking about you in the fast lane and the rest of us in… (*Struggling.*) the other lane.

MARGOT. What?

BRYAN. You asking not what you can do for your country, and us… (*Struggling.*) asking what not we can ask of said country but our country asking what it can do for us.

TESS. *Focus, Bryan.*

BRYAN. Tess – she's a good woman, Margot, but you wore away at her, wore away at her and belittled her for doing the hardest darn job in the world: *matricide.* (*Confused, but pushing on.*) You told her she was stupid for not finishing her degree, as if that was going to change the world. You know, self-esteem is the buzzword, Margot. That's what we're all trying to give our kids. A healthy dose of self-esteem – it's what anchors each of us in the ocean of existential despair – and that's an ocean with serious waves, Margot – and winds – winds and waves… *and* rocks. But you didn't buy that, did you, Margot? *Au confrère.* Every chance you got, you told her she couldn't swim, couldn't even get her Junior Certificate. And *every single thing* that Tess has troubling at her is due to one single fact and that is the question mark that hangs over her head. (*Beat.*) *Her father.*

MARGOT. *Irrelevant!*

TESS. Not to me!

MARGOT. A couple of anonymous little commas! Nobody. Nothing. An irrelevancy.

TESS. I look at myself as a mother and how hopeless I am and I think, well, look how I was mothered!

MARGOT. Honestly, you Generation Xs – you never stop whining about your parents. We didn't need our parents to tell us who we were.

TESS. Because you had real mothers. Ours were too busy finding themselves!

BRYAN. Well, I don't know about that, Margot. What I do know is that you've made it awfully complicated for the guys.

MARGOT. Oh, boo hoo.

BRYAN. I'm not saying you haven't made your mark, but I'm just wondering if we weren't all guinea pigs in a little experiment! You've *emasculated* us. (*Delighted by this word.*) It's been a process of *emasculation*. Oh, yessirree… Margot Mason has always been pretty damn good at the old routine.

TESS. Bryan, I appreciate you, I do. But I don't love you.

BRYAN. Oh, Tess. Don't say that.

TESS. Bryan, I don't love you.

BRYAN. Come on, Tess. We've got… (*Tiny beat as he recalls.*) three beautiful kids. We'll figure things out.

TESS. I'm so confused! I don't know who I am! I'm just an exhausted, miserable, empty woman with a question mark at the centre of her identity!

BRYAN. You are a good mother, Tess. You just need a little time to get to know who *you* are.

MOLLY. Are you sure you're not in love with him?

TESS. Certain.

BRYAN. I can understand that. I'm not a very exciting person and I think in your heart you know that what you want is someone with what people in the know call an 'edge'. I think you should follow your dreams, Tess.

MOLLY. Remarkable!

BRYAN. Not really, Molly. It's just that when you really love someone, you must set them free. Besides, Tess hankers for someone who's cooler than me, someone pretty wild, someone who likes Coldplay. Don't get me wrong, there is a small coolish element in me, but I'm not your full-blown cool-cat. That might surprise you.

MOLLY. I actually think Tess needs to do something outside of the domestic sphere.

BRYAN. Couldn't agree more.

MOLLY. Flex her muscles a little bit, get out in the world of big ideas.

BRYAN. That's exactly what I think. She's just not happy.

MOLLY. She's not happy.

BRYAN. She hasn't been happy for years.

MOLLY. I can see that.

BRYAN. You can see it in her face.

MOLLY. It's transparent.

BRYAN. She's always had something –

MOLLY. Just trying to –

BRYAN. That's right!

MOLLY. Free itself –

BRYAN. I think she's very creative –

MOLLY. Oh, me too –

MARGOT. Oh, excuse me interrupting this personality workshop, but –

BRYAN. We're only saying that Tess really needs to spread her wings, intellectually.

MARGOT. Isn't that what I've been saying all these years? Only, I'm a hard-line bitch for saying it.

BRYAN. It's the *place* you say these things *from*, Margot. You always say everything from *your* point of view.

MARGOT *registers the stupidity of this.*

TESS. You wanted me to be a professional because it would make *you* look good. You wanted me to live out your propaganda! I had three small children and how often did you babysit?

MARGOT. I'm not to blame for everything that's gone wrong in your lives. I'm a thinker! *It's my job to think.* Has it ever occurred to any of you that there was a generation of men and women who didn't wake up in the morning and wonder how the day was going to pan out for *them*, but leapt out of bed intent on figuring out how the world was going to pan out for *everybody*? I happened to get famous and now you're going to use my *fame* against me because you're not happy with yourselves? *Why don't you take a little responsibility and while you're at it, show a tiny bit of ordinary gratitude?*

MOLLY. You can't *demand* gratitude!

MARGOT. I fucking *earned* it!

Beat.

TESS. Well, that's all very well, but *who's my father*?

MARGOT. Tess, *when* are you going to let this go?

TESS. *Who is he?!*

MARGOT. I don't know!

TESS. Think!

Long beat as MARGOT *resolves at last to say what she has refused to admit for years.*

MARGOT. All right! Are you ready for this? Because you're not going to like it! It was a wild drunken party on the King's Road. It was the night Mick broke up with Marianne Faithfull. Marianne was covered in taramasalata. Joni Mitchell was off her face on Quaaludes and there were so many strobe lights going off, I've no idea who I was with! There were fifty virile young men there and one of them unzipped my Ossie Clark and lo and behold, I *conceived*. It was a dark fumble underneath a filthy hippy bedspread to the tune of 'Mrs Robinson'.

TESS. That's it! *That's it?*

The doorbell goes. Everyone freezes.

MOLLY. It's the police! Everyone shut up! Shut up! I'm warning you that if we're stormed by the police, I'm killing everyone in the name of my mother.

BRYAN (*with admiration*). Gosh!

FRANK, *an attractive, very masculine young man in his early thirties, appears at the French doors.*

MOLLY. Who are you?

TESS. It's the taxi driver!

FRANK. Oh, it's the big tipper!

TESS. You expect me to *reward* you for boring me to death?

FRANK. I was *sharing*. Sharing my life with you!

TESS. Your wife left you. Boo hoo.

FRANK. You weren't even listening!

TESS. It was all 'me, me, me'! What about me?

FRANK. What? *Me?*

TESS. *No. Me.*

FRANK. I opened up to you! Did you listen? Did you say, '*Frank, I acknowledge your pain*'? Did you manage a tiny little tip?

TESS. I paid you to drive, not talk!!

FRANK. Oh, lovely! Oh, that's right! A civil little conversation is going to kill you!

TESS. It wasn't a conversation, it was a very long monologue about a life where nothing's ever turned out right. I don't need to listen to that shit. *I'm living it!*

FRANK. Oh, that's right. Even *my* life is all about *you*.

MOLLY *waves the gun around.*

MOLLY. Sorry to interrupt but, I'm afraid, *neither* of you is the issue here.

FRANK. She's got a gun.

BRYAN. She has, Frank. It's a lethal weapon.

FRANK (*not unimpressed*). A chick with a gun!

MOLLY (*to* FRANK). I'm getting ready to shoot you.

FRANK (*indicating* TESS). Why don't you shoot *her* instead?

MARGOT. At last, a bit of common sense!

FRANK (*to* TESS). I *confided* in you!

TESS. Talky-talky talk-talk. Here's some advice from the female front line, honey, why don't you stop talking and *act*.

MARGOT. Marvellous!

FRANK. Oh, that's right, you girls go on about how men need to communicate, and then the moment we open up, you knock us down.

TESS. Jesus! You've had the upper hand for thousands of years, you've been to the moon while we stayed home and baked biscuits, you get to pee standing up and you're still not happy!

FRANK. Actually, I was talking to you as a human being, not as a female. Accept my apologies!

TESS (*stressed*). Listen, I've had a lot of bad experiences with taxi drivers and their personal reflections, okay? All right? *'The world's unjust.' 'I've got a great idea for a novel.' 'My wife doesn't understand me…'* I've heard it all before, buddy. *Comprendez?*

FRANK. She wanted me to be just like *her*. Sensitive, caring, a hands-on parent. She wanted me to access the feminine side, to listen, to open up, to be emotionally available and – and –

BRYAN (*lending a hand*). 'On the same page' —

FRANK. On the same page. So I was.

TESS. Good for you.

FRANK. I tried. I really tried. I stopped myself from holding my feelings in. I taught myself to see her as an equal partner in the venture of togetherness.

BRYAN. Wow.

FRANK. I let *her* make the decisions. I learnt to bake. When she had a problem, I *listened*. I didn't try to find a *solution* like any normal arsehole would. I did the laundry. I tried to let her drive without making scared noises even when she had the foot on the brake and the accelerator at the same time. When we got lost, I asked for directions. I watched cancer movies with her and cried. I was a beautiful, beautiful caring man.

BRYAN. Even I'm attracted, Frank!

FRANK. But, guess what? Once she had a man who was just like a woman, she realised what she really wanted was a man.

BRYAN. Typical!

TESS. Oh.

FRANK. So now I'm just going to be true to myself. Are you listening?

TESS. Okay, I'm listening!

FRANK. *I'm going to be the man I always was and had to hide!*

TESS. Okay! Okay!

FRANK. I'm going to be me, all right? Have you got it? *No more Mr Nice Guy!*

TESS. Actually, I –

FRANK. Sit down.

TESS. But I – I –

FRANK. Sit.

TESS. I'm not –

FRANK (*commanding*). I said, *sit down*.

MOLLY. Hold on –

TESS. Well, I –

FRANK. *Shut up and listen!*

> TESS *is mind-blown by this – it's the kind of manly behaviour she's been dreaming of. Her whole attitude to* FRANK *shifts.*

I trusted you. I needed to come back and tell you.

TESS. You needed to tell me – ?

FRANK. We're hurting.

TESS (*suddenly sympathetic*). Of course you are.

FRANK. I thought you'd understand.

TESS (*seeing him differently*). Well – I can see now that you might have had something to say…

FRANK. It's an incredible story about a man forced to live a lie. It's moving. It's deep.

MOLLY. Listen, this is my –

TESS (*growingly flirtatious and coy*). Well, possibly if I hadn't judged you so hastily I would have found that you were… riveting.

FRANK. Didn't seem like you were listening.

TESS. Underneath it all, I'm sure I *was* riveted. I was just exhausted.

BRYAN. She was exhausted, Frank. Bone tired. She wasn't in a mood to be rivettable.

MOLLY. I've got a gun!

MARGOT. Oh yes! Yes! Because men *are* so riveting! That's right!

FRANK. Hey!

MOLLY. *Is anybody listening to me?*

MARGOT. You think if you do a couple of loads of washing that makes you 'the new man'? The arrogance of it! We're not stupid! We know you'll try any performance piece to keep us barefoot and pregnant.

BRYAN. Oh, Margot, rest assured, I don't know any man who wants to get you... (*His nerve failing*.) barefoot.

MARGOT (*to* FRANK). Young man, you need to take a long hard look at yourself. You're the perfect example of how I've failed! How much work I have yet to do.

FRANK. Yeah? Well, you could start with the cow on your doorstep.

TESS (*laughs too loudly, smitten*). 'The cow on your doorstep'!

FRANK *takes in* MARGOT. *He's suddenly put it all together.*

FRANK. I recognise you! You're that old lady who's always annoying somebody!

MOLLY. Just about everybody!

MARGOT. Old? I'm just coming into myself, baby!

FRANK. I remember seeing you on TV. Banging on about what women want and how men are just great big losers...

MARGOT. Really? *Me?*

FRANK. You were rude. Very, very rude.

BRYAN. *Very.*

MOLLY. Shut up and listen!

MARGOT. Didn't like what I had to say, hey? Tiny bit *threatened*, were you?

FRANK. Where do you get off?

MARGOT. I don't get off, honey. That's the whole thing about Margot Mason. She's on the case 24/7, letting clowns like you know the world is changing even if you're not!

FRANK (*quietly furious*). Did you call me a clown?

MARGOT. Yes, cowboy, I did.

FRANK. Right!

FRANK *grabs the gun from an unsuspecting* MOLLY. *Screams all round.* FRANK *waves it in the air, pacing the room. They all hit the floor, suddenly terrified.*

Everyone on the floor!

He realises they're already on the floor.

Get your heads down! If anyone tries anything, I pull the trigger!

MOLLY. That's my gun! I went to a lot of trouble to get it!

FRANK (*pacing, pulling off his jacket*). Get your heads down or I'll pull the trigger! Something about you lot has made me... *snap*.

TESS (*excited*). He's snapped! He's snapped!

FRANK. At first I was just irritated but then I realised I'd *snapped*! I walk in here to give her a piece of my mind and within seconds I've got this ballbreaker driving me *right to the edge of sanity*.

MOLLY (*indignant*). This is *my* hostage situation!

FRANK (*fierce*). *I've got a lot of pain*. Okay? All right? Are you reading me?

MOLLY (*backing down*). I'm reading you!

FRANK. Are you reading me?

MOLLY. I'm reading you!

FRANK (*to all of them*). Oh yes, I'm good enough for you when it's raining, when the buses are on strike. I'm good enough for you when your shoes hurt and you want someone to get you from A to B. When I offer you the privilege of hearing about *my* life, *my* times, *my* soul... You just smirk...

TESS. You're right.

FRANK. Listening is the first step towards healing.

TESS. That's lovely, Frank.

BRYAN. Bro, let's just talk it through, man to man.

MARGOT (*droll*). That's funny!

FRANK. Oh, you're full of it, aren't you, lady? But you know what? You've got no idea *what* you're talking about. I'll tell you what women want: they want a *man*.

MARGOT. They've been brainwashed to think they want a man.

MOLLY. No, they've been brainwashed to think they *don't* want a man!

MARGOT. Are we talking feminist, post-feminist or post-post-feminist?

FRANK. *We're talking tying you to a post-post in a minute and organising some kindling.* You know, back when the sexes coexisted in caves, it was still the guys that took the rubbish out. Ever think about that?

BRYAN. Touché, Frank!

FRANK. You think Neanderthal man got around in rubber gloves?

BRYAN. Not on your life, bro!

FRANK. Men stood around the continental shelf – before it shifted – and had a little powwow with the chicky-boo: 'You want to clean the fridge?' And she said, 'Oh yes, I can clean the fridge better than you so that makes sense.' 'What about the light bulbs?' 'Well, I can do light bulbs if you do meaningless furniture-arranging.'

BRYAN. It worked for everyone.

FRANK. And then what? We hit the seventies and suddenly an arrangement that has worked perfectly well for thousands of years isn't good enough for the girls! No. Suddenly they know better. So some of the *ugly* ones launch a little experiment, and what happens? I'll tell you what happens!

BRYAN. Oh, good!

FRANK. Men find *that women do not feel passionately aroused by nice guys*. (*Beat*.) They still want the caveman. (*Beat*.) Women want a man who knows how to do two things for them really, really well: (*Beat*.) Foreplay. And tax.

TESS. Wow. The man's a sage!

BRYAN. He's certainly something of an historian.

MARGOT. You know, women don't just lie down and take this stuff any more!

TESS. I'm lying down and I'm taking it!

FRANK. Back off, lady!

MARGOT. Back off?

FRANK. Back off!

MARGOT. *In case you hadn't noticed, I'm handcuffed to the desk, you fucking imbecile.*

FRANK. I've got a lot of anger.

MOLLY *and* TESS. Who hasn't?!

FRANK. Life hasn't delivered.

MARGOT. No, well, guess what? There are no deliveries on *life*, you have to pick it up at the depot, you know what I'm saying? You babies don't know how to get on without everything being *given* to you! *You're all spoiled brats.* Go on, shoot me, but that's the truth! Talk about the 'me generation'! All this nonsense about personal identity and self-growth and being fulfilled! What a load of self-indulgent crap –

FRANK. Well, aren't you a smarty-pants!

MARGOT. Actually, yes. Yes, I am. I'm a Major Smarty-Pants, unlike you because your brain, unfortunately, is located in your dick!

FRANK. Well, Ms Smarty-Pants, my brain is actually too large for my penis!

TESS (*consoling and certain*). Oh, I'm sure that's not true...

BRYAN. I don't think size is the issue.

FRANK (*picking up*). What I do know is that there are some women who need to be told a thing or two. (*To* MARGOT.) You could do a lot worse than spend a few days taking care of a man!

BRYAN (*exhilarated*). Ho... ho... ho!

FRANK. You need to spend some time in a house with some testy-oster-test-est –

BRYAN (*quick to assist*). *Toblerone.*

FRANK. *Men. Pleasing* them. Let a man be a man!

BRYAN (*having the time of his life*). Woo-hoo!

MARGOT. Well, with your intellect, I can see why you're driving a taxi!

THEO REYNOLDS, *a dapper, handsome, sixty-year-old, comes through the French doors.*

FRANK. Get your hands up!

MOLLY. Who are you?

THEO. I'm Theo. I'm Margot's publisher. Who are you?

MOLLY. I'm her... home intruder.

THEO. Uh-huh. (*Indicating* FRANK.) And who are you?

TESS. He's the Messiah.

THEO (*surprised*). Not exactly what I imagined.

TESS. Frank's tired of feminism. He's snapped.

THEO. Who's Frank?

FRANK. Me. I've snapped.

THEO. Mags, what's going on here? (*Noticing.*) Are they *handcuffs*?

MARGOT. Yes, Theo.

THEO. This *is* looking like fun. What does *he* want?

BRYAN (*fast*). Frank's taxi is in the driveway. He drove Tess from the station because she couldn't handle the noise. The kids ate nine mothballs while I was in Dubai. Frank's wife led him down the garden path and he's hurting. Tess didn't listen because he was a taxi driver. He came back out of self-respect but now he's going to murder Margot.

THEO (*understanding the important part*). Murder Margot? But that's absurd. If Margot didn't exist, we'd have to invent her.

BRYAN *lunges for the gun which he successfully grabs from* FRANK.

BRYAN. It's okay. It's all okay. I've got the gun.

TESS, MARGOT *and* MOLLY (*with absolute terror*). *Bryan's got the gun!*

BRYAN (*with swagger*). We're all fine. Everything's under control because this little baby and me are old frie –

The gun goes off, hitting a vase, which explodes. Everybody screams, none longer, louder and more girlier than BRYAN *himself, who has thrown himself on the floor.*

BRYAN. AAARGHHHHHHHH!

In the chaos, MOLLY *grabs the gun from* BRYAN.

MOLLY. Okay, everybody hit the floor!

No one hits the floor.

THEO. What does *she* want?

MOLLY. I said, hit the floor!

No one moves.

TESS. Molly is here to murder Mum, too. (*Beat.*) We all are.

MOLLY. *Hello??!!!!* How come, when *he* says, 'Hit the floor,' everyone jumps and when I say it, nobody does anything? It's completely sexist.

TESS. It *is* sexist. But to be honest, it's also just about being *commanding*.

THEO (*with urgency*). Young lady, I don't know what your grievance is, but you must not, under any circumstances, kill this woman!

MARGOT (*with affection*). Theo!

MOLLY. Give me one good reason!

THEO. If she goes, Reynolds and Purbrick goes down the drain.

MARGOT (*appalled*). Theo!

THEO. The bank is breathing down my neck. We haven't published a best-seller since *The Islamic Vagina*. We're in serious trouble. If she doesn't finish the book by next week the company's finished!

MARGOT. So I'm just a cash ambulance to you, Theo. After all these years!

THEO. Of course not, Mags. You're my dearest, oldest friend. But the fact is, we need you alive. Only you can pull us back from the brink.

MARGOT (*pleased*). Only me?

THEO. You're the only one that can save us!

MARGOT. Stick that in your pipe, La Paglia!

THEO. None of you has any idea of the catastrophe facing us. Small publishers are fighting for their lives! The marketplace is this vast, all-consuming monster, hungry for vulgarity. Do we need Jason Timberlake's biography?

BRYAN. That's a hard one.

THEO. I'm a man of immense and noble taste but I'm struggling for air in an era of unadulterated crudity. It's all about marketing now. Who needs content when you have marketing?

BRYAN (*confused, in agreement*). Content's overrated. Always has been. Always will be.

THEO. The multinationals are moving in and Margot's our last chance. She's my J.K. Rowling and she has to churn them out *fast*.

BRYAN. Who's her Harry Potter, Theo?

THEO. A – a – *vagina*, Bryan. If I can get the book out there in the next five months, we have a chance but *time is of the essence*. How much have you written, Mags?

MOLLY. Two-hundred-and-twenty-three words!

THEO. Oh fuck!

MARGOT. For God's sake, I'd be working right now, if this
woman hadn't handcuffed me!

THEO. Can't you type with handcuffs on?

MARGOT. Listen, Theo, *The Female of the Species is* going to
be a best-seller, if only you'd all leave me alone!

THEO. *Female of the Species.* Not bad.

MOLLY. I thought of it.

THEO (*thinking*). Maybe a cover with good-looking girls…
shopping.

FRANK. That would work.

MARGOT. I'm just a punching bag for everyone's self-pity!
Does anyone have any feelings for me at all? Or is it all
just about what *I* can do for *you*? Here I am, experiencing
one of the greatest crises in my life, and who is here for
me? No one!

THEO. What crisis?

MARGOT (*despairing*). What's it all for, Theo? What's it all
for?

THEO. It's for Umbria, Mags! It's for first-class travel and
lovely little etchings at Sotheby's! Keep your eye on the ball!

MARGOT. It's not the money, Theo! It's having a valuable
place in the universe! My life has been carved out by *The
Cerebral Vagina*, but that was written thirty-five years ago!
Who am I, Theo?

THEO. Who are you?

MARGOT. Apart from a provocative, ballsy, searing intellect?
Apart from that, *who am I*?

MOLLY (*to MARGOT, gathering momentum*). Don't you see?
Don't you understand? You have this remarkable power, this
remarkable ability to look at the world critically – but it's no

good having power for the sake of power, it *must* be a force for good. You need to understand that human beings are frail and complex, that the imagination is more powerful than the purely rational – that ideology denies the true, strange beauty of the human experience.

Pause as everyone takes in this passionate treatise.

THEO. Wow!

FRANK. Damn!

TESS. Oh!

BRYAN (*to* THEO). Isn't she something?

THEO (*with wonderment*). Where did she come from?!

BRYAN. It's a long story. But in a nutshell: abandoned at birth, did nude modelling, worked in croissant shop, found birth mother, dead under train clutching *Cerebral Vagina*, waitressed in Moroccan café, felt up by owner, wanted to be writer, humiliated by Margot, decided to kill her.

THEO. *Sensational!*

FRANK. I can help you, Margot.

MARGOT. I don't need your help!

FRANK. I think you do. I can liberate you, Margot. I can free you from your fear.

MARGOT. I have no fear!

FRANK. Why is it you can't write your book? What is it you're burdened by?

MARGOT (*faltering*). I'm burdened by constant interruptions, for one thing!

FRANK. I think that in your heart of hearts you know that your writer's block is about terror, Margot. The terror of facing the truth about yourself. Down there, in the deepest recesses of your inner being, certainty is breaking up into a thousand tiny pieces...

MARGOT (*suddenly and uncharacteristically uncertain*). It is?

FRANK. And the full, wondrous weirdness of *you* is waiting to express itself. You need to be open.

MARGOT. Well... Well, perhaps...

FRANK. You have to let people in, Margot. *The Cerebral Vagina* is out there in the universe and it's doing just fine without you.

MARGOT (*realising*). Of course it is...

FRANK. All the many battles you've fought and won, the great strides in thinking that have changed things for ever... let them be.

MARGOT. Let them be?

FRANK. And return for a moment to the *self*, Margot. The chick within. Think how freeing it will be to let the world look after itself, let others take responsibility, let go and return your gaze to the core of Margot Matron.

MARGOT. Mason.

FRANK. Mason. You need to explore your own potential again. See yourself as a blank canvas. Be curious instead of certain. Acknowledge the full burden of loving others and being loved.

MARGOT. Me?

FRANK. Sure! People do love you, Margot.

MARGOT (*sniff*). They do?

FRANK. Of course they do, I could feel it the moment I walked into the room. In your own way, you all love her, don't you?

He looks at everyone for confirmation. They very subtly acknowledge that they do, indeed, feel, if not love, then a strange affection for MARGOT, *after all.*

MARGOT *takes this as good enough. She looks at* MOLLY.

MARGOT. Here I was fixated on this selfless mission, this global endeavour to wake up the world to how much better it could be and *of course I did*, because helping others is what comes so naturally to me. But how right you are, Frank. I can't carry that weight on my shoulders any more. My God. Isn't that just typical! When wisdom finally arrives, it comes in the form of the idiot savant –

FRANK. Just a –

BRYAN. It's a compliment, Frank. It means *knowing* idiot.

FRANK. Well, I –

MARGOT. *The next chapter has to be all about me.* All about nurturing the deepest part of myself, down, down, down (*Beat.*) – *down* beneath the ego. I can forgive. I can let go. And accept the quaint fallibility of human nature with grace and... elegance and tolerance. (*Turning.*) Tess...

TESS *looks at her expectantly.*

Tess, I do...

TESS. Yes?

MARGOT. I do...

TESS. Yes?

MARGOT (*not quite reformed enough*). You know.

Beat.

Molly, I'm not responsible for your mother. But I am sorry.

Beat.

MOLLY. Thank you, Margot.

MOLLY *puts the keys to the handcuffs on the desk.*

THEO. Now that the epiphanies are over... Is there anything to eat?

MOLLY. I'll pop into the kitchen, but if anyone tries anything, I'll – be very annoyed.

FRANK *picks up the keys from the desk and unlocks the handcuffs as* MOLLY *and* BRYAN *exit.* MARGOT, *newly liberated, takes a second to peruse* FRANK's *very attractive body.*

BRYAN. Do you need a hand?

MOLLY (*coyly*). Thank you, Bryan.

TESS (*urgent, impassioned*). Excuse me! Hello! *I'm* still wracked with pain.

FRANK. You need to move on, babe.

TESS. Don't you think I've tried – Frankie? I've tried and I've tried, but every time I want to liberate the child within, I'm faced with the deep crevasse of an identity-free zone.

THEO. You need a distraction, Tess. A book!

TESS. I'd love to do that, Theo. But I can't write a word until I know who was standing on the footpath at the outset of my own personal journey.

MARGOT (*new, improved*). That's a beautiful phrase, Tess.

MOLLY *and* BRYAN *re-enter, carrying a tray with dip, and laughing.*

BRYAN. We found some things in the fridge. Some very good taramasalata.

THEO. Oh, good. (*Helping himself.*) Taramasalata, eh? For some strange reason, it always makes me think of Marianne Faithfull.

MARGOT, TESS, BRYAN *and* MOLLY *all freeze.* THEO *continues to help himself and eat.*

Excellent. Is this yours, Mags?

TESS (*tremulously*). Did you say Marianne Faithfull?

THEO *stops eating mid-bite, realising the strange impact he is having.*

THEO. No idea why. Some strange association. Doesn't make much sense.

Long beat.

TESS. *Daddy!!*

Long beat. It dawns on THEO.

THEO (*to* MARGOT). Could it be so?

MARGOT. Surely not.

THEO. Is it possible – ?

MARGOT. Were you there that night, Theo? That night on the King's Road when –

THEO. Mick split with Marianne?

Sharp intake of breath from MARGOT.

I was *there*, Mags. Tripping the light fantastic!

MARGOT (*shocked*). *You were?*

THEO. *Everyone* was there. You looked ravishing in Ossie Clark –

MARGOT. But you were already out of the closet!

THEO. No, darling, I was hovering in the doorway of the *armoire*. No one could have resisted you.

MARGOT (*touched*). Theo…

THEO. I never realised that that was the night –

THEO *looks at* TESS.

My dear, dear, girl!

TESS *rushes over to* THEO *and hugs him.*

TESS. I'm feeling a surge of power! A surge of meaning and fulfilment. For the first time in years, I feel capable of anything!

THEO. I'm a father! A *father*.

BRYAN (*shaking his hand*). Congratulations.

THEO. Oh, this is marvellous! You'll be able to come to me and Adrian's for access weekends! (*Turning his sights to* MOLLY.) In the meantime, Molly, I'd like to offer you a contract.

MOLLY. What?

THEO. Personal memoir, tragedy at the heart, needing 'closure'…

MOLLY. You think I can write?

BRYAN. You can do anything, Molly!

THEO. Your difficult life, being given away, your mother impaled on a copy of *The Cerebral Vagina*.

MOLLY. Yes, yes! Only, my mother wasn't impaled on *The Cerebral Vagina*. She was holding it when she fell under a train.

THEO (*sternly*). She was *impaled*, Molly. *On the spine. It was a hardback!*

MOLLY (*learning fast*). Yes, oh yes, it's coming back to me. She was impaled.

THEO (*to* FRANK). And as for you, young man…

BRYAN. Yes!

THEO. There is one small possibility. The post-post-post-feminist take on the female experience, the one thing we haven't had: a groundbreaking work that will transform the publishing industry for a decade and fill the Sunday papers. The sock-it-back response, the *vive-la-différence* response, the unexpected, highly provocative, intellectualised anti-intellectual, the '*stuff it, let's talk sense*' angle, the anti-metrosexual, the '*had it up to here but yet the concerned, kind and helpful*' response, the handsome, young, virile *male* response to what a woman needs…

FRANK. *The Female of the Species*.

MARGOT. How nice. The whole world is writing a book, all except me, the *real* writer. I'll just sit here all alone with my writer's block for company while you all scramble for your Apple Macs. (*Picking up the copy of* The Cerebral Vagina.) Sometimes I really have to wonder what this book has really done for me. It's been a chain around my neck. And yet, if it weren't for this book, society would have doddled along complacently, never searching for the deeper truths, comforted by its own insufferable laziness. *I changed the world.* I did it then. *And I can fucking do it again.* (*Beat. Finally inspired.*) Hold on… Hold on… I've got a flicker of…

perhaps something that… An idea for the book I can…
Something's coming! Something's coming! Something that
sends me *and* feminism where we've never been before! A
completely new take on the Margot Mason oeuvre! A stun-
ning divergence! A mindblowingly original concept!

Beat.

The Vulnerable Vagina.

She hurls The Cerebral Vagina *across the room.*

Feminism… and Love!

The book lands on the gun which immediately fires.

MARGOT *collapses.*

Shocked silence as they all move forward to take in
MARGOT*'s seemingly lifeless body. Finally:*

TESS. *Oh. My. (God.)*

MARGOT *sits bolt upright. The others draw back, shocked.*
MARGOT *looks down and finds that her heart has been*
covered by the enormous tome, Men Are Awful, *which has*
absorbed the bullet. She lifts it gingerly off herself.

MARGOT. *Men Are Awful.* It took the bullet! I suppose I should
be grateful to the male species for saving my life, since if
they weren't so awful, I wouldn't have written the book.

THEO (*relieved*). That's my Margot.

MARGOT. I've been hounded by the patriarchy, attacked by the
establishment, sabotaged by competitors, savaged by
narrow-minded sexist bigots and finally *shot. There's nothing*
they can do to Margot Mason that will keep her down.

TESS. *The Vulnerable Vagina.* That's lovely.

MARGOT. Is anyone hungry?

MOLLY. We could eat outside!

MARGOT. There's some very nice figs and prosciutto…

BRYAN. Shall we set the table, Molly?

MOLLY. Absolutely, Bryan!

THEO. I could eat a horse!

BRYAN. Oh, there's a *cow* on the doorstep, Theo. I'm sure we could...

The lights fade to a beautiful evening, as they happily begin to organise a meal.

Blackout.

The End.